Conjugal Rites

A Comedy in Two Acts

by Roger Hall

A Samuel French Acting Edition

New York Hollywood London Toronto

SAMUELFRENCH.COM

Copyright © 1990, 1992 by Roger Hall

ALL RIGHTS RESERVED

CAUTION: Professionals and amateurs are hereby warned that *CONJUGAL RITES* is subject to a Licensing Fee. It is fully protected under the copyright laws of the United States of America, the British Commonwealth, including Canada, and all other countries of the Copyright Union. All rights, including professional, amateur, motion picture, recitation, lecturing, public reading, radio broadcasting, television and the rights of translation into foreign languages are strictly reserved. In its present form the play is dedicated to the reading public only.

The amateur live stage performance rights to *CONJUGAL RITES* are controlled exclusively by Samuel French, Inc., and licensing arrangements and performance licenses must be secured well in advance of presentation. PLEASE NOTE that amateur Licensing Fees are set upon application in accordance with your producing circumstances. When applying for a licensing quotation and a performance license please give us the number of performances intended, dates of production, your seating capacity and admission fee. Licensing Fees are payable one week before the opening performance of the play to Samuel French, Inc., at 45 W. 25th Street, New York, NY 10010.

Licensing Fee of the required amount must be paid whether the play is presented for charity or gain and whether or not admission is charged.

Stock licensing fees quoted upon application to Samuel French, Inc.

For all other rights than those stipulated above, apply to: Casarotto Ramsay, Waverly House, 7-12 Noel Street, London W1F 3GQ England.

Particular emphasis is laid on the question of amateur or professional readings, permission and terms for which must be secured in writing from Samuel French, Inc.

Copying from this book in whole or in part is strictly forbidden by law, and the right of performance is not transferable.

Whenever the play is produced the following notice must appear on all programs, printing and advertising for the play: "Produced by special arrangement with Samuel French, Inc."

Due authorship credit must be given on all programs, printing and advertising for the play.

No one shall commit or authorize any act or omission by which the copyright of, or the right to copyright, this play may be impaired.

No one shall make any changes in this play for the purpose of production.

Publication of this play does not imply availability for performance. Both amateurs and professionals considering a production are strongly advised in their own interests to apply to Samuel French, Inc., for written permission before starting rehearsals, advertising, or booking a theatre.

No part of this book may be reproduced, stored in a retrieval system, or transmitted in any form, by any means, now known or yet to be invented, including mechanical, electronic, photocopying, recording, videotaping, or otherwise, without the prior written permission of the publisher.

ISBN 978-0-573-69308-3   Printed in U.S.A.   #5252

IMPORTANT BILLING AND CREDIT REQUIREMENTS

All producers of CONJUGAL RITES *must* give credit to the Author of the Play in all programs distributed in connection with performances of the Play and in all instances in which the title of the Play appears for purposes of advertising, publicizing or otherwise exploiting the Play and/or a production. The name of the Author *must* also appear on a separate line, on which no other name appears, immediately following the title, and *must* appear in size of type not less than fifty percent the size of the title type.

Conjugal Rites was first performed in the UK at the Palace Theatre on January 24, 1991. It starred Nicky Henson and Gwen Taylor.

Conjugal Rites was also performed in New Zealand at the Fortune Theatre. It starred Timothy Bartlett and Janet Fisher.

CHARACTERS

BARRY, late forties/fifty.

GEN(evieve), a few years younger than Barry.

CONJUGAL RITES

A bedroom furnished in some style. (Gen claims the bedroom needs redecorating but this is not readily discernible.
A desk, TV with remote control. They each have separate built-in wardrobes. An ensuite bathroom. At least one good painting.
Cordless phone is by Gen's side of the bed. It has an answering machine attached. Clock radio. Bedroom. DARK. Two BODIES in bed.
PHONE rings.
BARRY stirs. HE tries to focus on the digital clock.
GEN's hand reaches out for the phone, but it stops after FOUR RINGS.
BARRY settles back. HE then realizes it has been answered on other extension.
BARRY picks it up. Listens just a moment.

BARRY. Philip, I don't know who's calling you but tell them 7:15 on a Saturday morning is not the time to—Liverpool! I don't care if they are playing Arsenal, what about Law? You had to sit re-takes and here you are—I am not panicking, Philip. Whose car? When will you be back? I do have some rights—*(HE rings off.)*

(HE lies there. PHONE pings a moment later (i.e. Philip has rung off). BARRY lies awake and braces himself for

the front DOOR to slam. It does so.
A series of GRUNTS from under bedclothes, which HE interprets and answers.)

BARRY. Philip and his friend Steve off to Anfield.
GEN. GRUNT
BARRY. I don't know.
GEN. GRUNT
BARRY. I didn't ask. (*HE settles down.*) And Happy Anniversary.

(Cynical GRUNT from bedclothes.
BARRY tries to get back to sleep.)

GEN. (*Now awakened, won't go back to sleep.*) God, this room could do with re-decorating.
BARRY. (*Grunts.*) ... back to sleep ...
GEN. The paper's peeling.
BARRY. GRUNTS
GEN. Twenty-one years.
BARRY. A SURPRISED GRUNT. (Is it that long since the bedroom's been touched?)
GEN. How many couples do we know who've survived that long? Is there something wrong with us?
BARRY. QUERY GRUNT.
GEN. Twenty-one years of marriage. They should give us a tax break.
BARRY. Gen ... back to sleep.
GEN. What is twenty-one? Not silver or gold, or diamond. Is it glass? When I was girl, I knew all those.
BARRY. Back to sleep.
GEN. Isn't it embarrassing to look back all those years.

How could we live like that! Totally different world. You realize we could be together for another twenty-one years?

BARRY. Not if I don't get back to sleep.

GEN. If we're so different now from what we were then, how different will we be in another twenty-one years?

(SHE gets out of bed to push aside a curtain to see what sort of day it is. As a result, LIGHT hits BARRY's closed eyes.)

GEN. It's raining. You can go back to sleep—

BARRY. (*Over the above.*) I've asked you and asked you and asked you—don't pull those curtains—

GEN. I was seeing what sort of day it was.

BARRY. Pull some other curtains. That way the street light shines right on my face. Right on ...

GEN. Don't be silly, it's only a quick peep.

BARRY. Like a laser beam.

GEN. Pathetic.

BARRY. It's not much to ask. You just ignore it.

GEN. Anything else? While we're at it. What else bugs you, Barry, about me? How would you like me to change?

BARRY. Stop buying me jockey underpants.

GEN. What?

BARRY. They're uncomfortable.

GEN. I didn't know that.

BARRY. Just 'cause they look good on TV ads.

GEN. On some people they look good. What sort do you want?

BARRY. Boxer.

GEN. Boxer shorts don't look sexy, Barry.

BARRY. I've worn jockeys for years and Kathleen Turner hasn't been near me. Or Madonna.

GEN. But I have.

BARRY. I thought that was the after-shave you keep giving me.

GEN. I've got a list for you.

BARRY. List?

GEN. Of changes. For you to make. For us to get through the next twenty-one years.

BARRY. Empty the dishwasher.

GEN. Yes.

BARRY. Do the weekly shopping.

GEN. Only once a fortnight.

BARRY. Otherwise perfect.

GEN. A bladder that doesn't require the owner to get up two or three times every night.

BARRY. I don't enjoy it, Gen!

GEN. One thing you could do: don't flush the loo till you've finished peeing.

BARRY. Ah.

GEN. I can never work out why you do it.

BARRY. It saves time.

(PHONE goes.)

BARRY. Impacted wisdom.

GEN. Access dispute.

BARRY. They say that one of the definitions of middle age is when the phone rings you hope it's not for you.

GEN. *(Picks up the phone.)* Hallo. Yes it is. I see. Yes. *(Indicates to Barry she was right in her guess.)* I'm sure the kids weren't looking a mess—I'm sure he doesn't realize how much clothes cost these days. Well if he says shoes not cleaned is a sign of neglect, Barry says he would have been taken away from me long ago. No, my husband. It was a joke. Your children won't be taken away from you just because he says they're untidy. He's being a pain—he's getting at you. You know what they're like. I'll have a word with his solicitor. Your children are fine. Yes. Bye. (*RINGS off.*) God. What a lot of misery ...

BARRY. When you took Law, I had no idea you wanted to practice.

(*Pause. GEN looks depressed.*)

BARRY. I just thought you wanted to take Law.

GEN. Fighting with your kids is no fun, but fighting over them.

BARRY. Whereas I wanted to be a dentist. I didn't want to study dentistry.

GEN. You wanted to be a doctor.

BARRY. I wish my failing to get into a medical school could be wiped from your memory disc ...

GEN. Would you ever fight over the children?

BARRY. Only to make sure you got them.

GEN. Not now! WOULD you have? (*Pause.*) Would you?

BARRY. Yes. But it didn't happen. (*Trying to change the mood.*) I don't know if it should be glass, zinc or corrugated iron. It's just a present. Happy Anniversary. (*HE reaches under bed for wrapped present.*)

GEN. (*Still depressed. Before SHE has seen the present.*) Chocolates.

BARRY. (*Hurt.*) Yes.

GEN. It always is. (*Unwraps them.*) Ohhh! Your favorites.

(*THEY each have one. SHE hands him the one he always takes first.*)

GEN. You used to do a card as well. With one of your favorite quotes inside. You used to keep a notebook of bits of poetry you liked, remember?
BARRY. Those were the days I still read poetry.
GEN. You used to read it to me. I haven't seen that notebook around for ages.
BARRY. If you ever find it, let me know. Something I want to add to it.
GEN. What?
BARRY. Never mind.
GEN. Remember how we used to save the silver paper for the guide dogs?
BARRY. What those guide dogs wanted with silver paper, I shall never—
GEN. Fool. (*Sudden thought.*) How does it save you time!
BARRY. (*Mouthful of chocolate.*) Mm?
GEN. Flushing the loo while you're—it can't make the slightest difference.
BARRY. I know it doesn't, but I think it does.
GEN. It drives me crazy, Barry.
BARRY. From now on, I'll keep my spare hand in my pocket until I've finished. (*After a while.*) I notice you haven't bought me a present.
GEN. I'm taking us to dinner.
BARRY. Oh. Thank you. Where?

GEN. Pierre's.

BARRY. Oh.

GEN. What's wrong with it!

BARRY. Nothing, nothing.

GEN. What!

BARRY. Nothing!

GEN. Say (*What you mean*)! I think the food there's lovely.

BARRY. What there is of it.

GEN. What!

BARRY. It looks nice; but the sorbet is one of the bigger courses.

GEN. Fine. I'll cancel it.

BARRY. No.

GEN. Doesn't worry me.

BARRY. Don't be silly.

GEN. I don't mind.

BARRY. Gen, I shall be honored and delighted to be your guest tonight. Thank you very much. I'm touched.

GEN. Really?

BARRY. Yes.

GEN. I was hoping you'd be pleased.

BARRY. I am. (*HE gives her a kiss.*)

GEN. If we weren't married, who would it be? You always fancied Sheila.

BARRY. Sheila who?

GEN. Sheila White. My bridesmaid. I think she fancied you.

BARRY. Now you tell me.

GEN. She married a roofing contractor. He fell off eventually.

BARRY. I fancied her, but I didn't know she fancied

me!

GEN. She fancied everyone.

BARRY. I wonder what she's doing now.

GEN. Who was the first person you lusted after? Your first pin up?

BARRY. No.

GEN. Tell me.

BARRY. No

GEN. Tell me.

BARRY. No.

GEN. Oh come on.

(Pause.)

BARRY. Doris Day.

(GEN laughs and laughs.)

BARRY. I knew I shouldn't have told you. I was very young at the time.

GEN. One of your receptionists looked a bit like her! That explains it! You were always talking about her—

BARRY. All right, who have you fancied? Been smitten by anyone over the years? Apart from the gynecologist.

GEN. Everybody fell in love with him.

BARRY. Huh.

GEN. There are some distinguished older men around these days.

BARRY. Who?

GEN. Ah, well, George Selby, he's improved with age.

BARRY. Selby!! Dr. Selby! *(Sniggers.)*

GEN. He's grown old gracefully. Lovely grey hair.

BARRY. Huh! What about Gavin McGuire, MP. He gets the ladies' votes. You're always doing business with him.

GEN. (*Scorn.*) Him—he's got toothbrushes all over town!

BARRY. Has he?

GEN. Everybody knows that.

BARRY. I didn't know that. I don't know all these things! All over town?

GEN. That's what they say. (*SHE has another chocolate. Offers him one.*) Fancy a soft centre, Barry? Mm? (*SHE tries to entice him.*) Not going to waste your little op are we? Good money that cost us. (*Sings.*)
"Take me back to the black hills
The black hills of Dakota..."

BARRY. I knew I shouldn't have told you.

GEN. Take me, Rock Hudson.

BARRY. Yes, well, as we now know, that was most unlikely. Hadn't we better wait till Gillian leaves for music classes?

GEN. She knows.

BARRY. What?

GEN. She knows. That Saturday mornings sometimes we ...

BARRY. She told you!

GEN. Yes.

BARRY. I couldn't imagine my parents DOING it, let alone mention it to them.

GEN. Which generation do you prefer?

BARRY. I suppose you're right.

GEN. I think she was quite pleased. Half the kids at

school have only got one parent—

BARRY. Does she actually ... listen?

GEN. Yes—she has an inverted glass pressed against our wall. No! She heard us one Saturday morning. The bed.

BARRY. It's that headboard. It's always put me off. I wonder when my parents did it ...

GEN. People can still have sex in their nineties, you know.

BARRY. Not with the light on, surely.

GEN. The tragedy of old age is lusting after people and being able to do little about it.

BARRY. I've been like that for years.

GEN. Men! It's straight from adolescence to mid-life crisis.

BARRY. What am I supposed to have done?

GEN. I see it all in my work.

BARRY. I didn't have an adolescence, Gen, I was an only child. Rebellion for me was refusing to part my hair. Once I didn't do the lawn. I feel I've missed out.

GEN. No need to miss out now.

(HE moves towards her. THEY embrace. BARRY gives a squeal of pain. Back trouble! HE has to lie on his back to recover.)

GEN. Sometimes I get sick of your back.
BARRY. Sometimes I get sick of your front.
GEN. (*Furious.*) What do you mean!!!
BARRY. Nothing nothing.
GEN. You mean ... (*SHE looks at her breasts.*) They're not so bad.

BARRY. Just very familiar. Shall I tell Gillian the cabaret has been postponed?
GEN. Cancelled.
BARRY. She should be taking Toby for a walk. One of the conditions we got the dog.
GEN. I'll take him later.

(PHONE goes.)

GEN. Hallo. Hang on. (*Hands phone over to Barry. SHE gets out of bed, puts on dressing gown and goes out of the room.*)
BARRY. Leo! I'd love to come to Cardiff and watch them play England! Thanks a—second thoughts, perhaps not. Not wise on one's wedding anniversary. And Gen's taking me out tonight so ... Yes. Will you be down at the Old Boys tomorrow? Take you on at snooker. Great. See you then. Love to Pam.

(GEN returns with a national newspaper plus the local one. SHE gets back into bed.
BARRY reaches for the daily paper. SHE hands him the local rag.
EACH has to get glasses on.)

BARRY. (*Grunts.*) I see your court appearance last week made the Fourth Estate.
GEN. Which ...?
BARRY. Borough argues for rubbish dump. Mrs. G. M. Masefield ... see ... appearing for the Borough—

(GEN takes the paper off him to read it.)

BARRY. (*Makes sure he now gets the national newspaper.*) One of Edward Maxwell's cases he fobbed off on to you I suppose. Smarmy prick. Why you joined his firm I'll never—

GEN. Tch! They've put the case of those who are appealing in full—the Borough's side of it gets hardly a mention.

BARRY. I don't understand what you see in it all. It's mostly non molestation orders and menopausal shoplifters...

GEN. Better than rotten teeth and receding gums.

BARRY. True.

GEN. (*Flicks through the rest of the paper.*) Good grief! Good God! (*Starts giggling.*)

BARRY. What? (*HE makes a grab for that part of the paper.*)

GEN. Hold on. (*Giggles again.*)

BARRY. What!!

GEN. It's one of those anniversary messages. In the paper.

BARRY. GRUNTS

GEN. To us.

BARRY. What does it say?

GEN. "To Mum and Dad. Happy Anniversary ..."

BARRY. Could be worse.

GEN. It is—they've printed our wedding photo with it.

(*BARRY sits up in fury, has to collapse back with pain.*)

GEN. God, the short skirt!!!

BARRY. Look at me! My hair was longer than yours!

GEN. (*Still amused.*) It'll be on the notice board at work on Monday! "Will you, Stephen Barry take Genevieve Myra—"

BARRY. I'd forgotten how short skirts were. Yours is way above—

GEN. I know!

BARRY. Sheila White looked fantastic, as I recall. She had the legs.

GEN. She hasn't now.

BARRY. (*Sighs.*) The mini-skirt was nice while it lasted.

GEN. Not for women.

BARRY. You didn't complain at the time.

GEN. Women didn't then.

BARRY. You've made up for it since!

GEN. With good cause!

BARRY. Meaning?

GEN. You've only got to look at the Hoover to put your back out.

BARRY. I cook!

(*Front DOOR is heard slamming.*)

GEN. Gillian.

BARRY. (*Gets out of bed, lopes to the window hunched over like a hunchback, looks out.*) Gone.

(*HE goes to get back into bed, perhaps expectantly, but GEN is now up and has gone through to the bathroom. Leaves bathroom door open.*)

BARRY. (*Decides to stay up. Comes back to have a*

good look at the photo.) My hair was longer than yours.

GEN. (*From the bathroom.*) I'm going round to see Dad today. Want to come?

BARRY. I went last week.

GEN. What are your plans for the day?

BARRY. (*Whispers.*) Watch the rugby on telly. (*Out loud sighs.*) Go through the accounts. (*Indicating them on the desk.*)

GEN. Happy for me to do them all those years.

BARRY. I'm not complaining. Get some stuff ready for the next Old Boys meeting.

GEN. (*Comes out of the bathroom.*) The bloody Old Boys!

BARRY. We raise funds to get better amenities for the school. What's wrong with that!

GEN. And drink a lot of booze in the process. And old boys always have more money than old girls—

(*PHONE goes. GEN answers.*)

GEN. Hallo? Yes ... yes. Isn't it a scream! Don't we look frights? Barry didn't mind. Thought it a great joke. Twenty-one years. (*Laughs.*) Doesn't bear thinking about. (*Rings off.*) Does it.

Scene 2

Evening, same day.
The bedroom is empty.
Sound of lavatory FLUSHING.

BARRY enters from the bathroom. HE is in his underwear.

BARRY. I did it Gen! I didn't flush the loo until ...

(SHE isn't there.
BARRY gives some indication that underpants are uncomfortable. Rummages through the remaining chocolates [probably on the mantelpiece]. Decides there aren't enough left to risk it. HE goes to the desk, opens drawer, and moves something to reveal [deliberately hidden] a packet of chocolate biscuits. HE stuffs two in his mouth quickly. Picks up electric shaver. Starts to shave. Then pretends it is a microphone and becomes a singer.)

BARRY. (*Sings.*) Oh, I cain't get no satisfaction ...

(The performance develops. In his mind, there is now an audience, HE is putting more into it ...
GEN enters in dressing gown and sees his movements [but hasn't heard the words, which would have been a giveaway].)

GEN. Another adolescent fantasy, Barry?
BARRY. An every day one.
GEN. I don't know why I bother. Cooking her a tea. She said she'd rather have had fish and chips.
BARRY. (*Muttering.*) Not the only one.
GEN. What!!
BARRY. Nothing. Nothing.
GEN. If you'd rather not—
BARRY. Nothing. Delighted. Thrilled.

GEN. Fancy yourself with Dire Straits, do you?

BARRY. Mm? Forget it.

GEN. You'd enjoy being on stage in front of screaming fans, mm?

BARRY. Too right I would! It must be fantastic.

GEN. Any other heroes?

BARRY. Henry Miller and Georges Simenon.

GEN. You don't read either of them.

BARRY. When Henry Miller was in his seventies he went to Paris and went on a sexual rampage that lasted several years. Most days of his life, Georges Simenon had two or three women a day: not his wife.

GEN. I don't think either of them had bad backs, Barry.

BARRY. (*Goes to wardrobe.*) What am I going to wear (to this wretched place).

GEN. What exciting range have we got? (*SHE looks at his clothes in the wardrobe.*) One aging suit; one other suit you never wear; one sports jacket to be worn with roll-neck sweater or with sports shirt cheekily open and with gold chain if you had one over hairy chest if you had one.

BARRY. (*Irritated.*) What would you like me to wear! You're taking me.

GEN. (*Makes a selection and hands clothes to him.*) Have you finished Gillian's homework yet?

BARRY. Er ... which ...?

GEN. Nomadic tribes.

BARRY. Forgot.

GEN. It has to be in by Monday.

BARRY. Long time ago, deep down in the memory ... didn't it used to be the children did the homework?

GEN. It would never work. (*Maybe GEN is now at mirror putting on make-up. SHE sighs.*) Do you think

Dad's getting worse?

BARRY. Worse?

GEN. I tried to clean his place up a bit. He took it as a personal insult.

BARRY. He hates me doing the lawn.

GEN. Mrs. Harlow has said she'd be happy to go in and clean but he won't hear of it. He won't put the heaters on. I was freezing! I asked him what he does with the money that he doesn't spend on heat. 'Course he didn't answer.

BARRY. Yes, well we've got a good idea.

GEN. No, I think he's cut it out.

BARRY. Huh.

GEN. He has!

BARRY. The kids should go and see him more ...

GEN. They hate going. Have you eaten all the chocolates?

BARRY. No!

GEN. Most of them!

BARRY. If I don't eat something before hand, I'll die of starvation.

GEN. Tonight, try not to eat your bread roll and my bread roll before the soup arrives.

BARRY. I'm not sure this is a good idea.

GEN. What?

BARRY. Dinner—just the two of us. What are we going to talk about? I mean there is nothing left.

GEN. I'd assumed you'll talk about whether to trade up the car—

BARRY. OK! OK! As long as bedroom re-decorating isn't mentioned.

GEN. It needs it!

BARRY. The kitchen was four years in the making—

and that was before the builders even started. And I still don't like it.

GEN. How would you know, you're hardly ever in it.

BARRY. Here we go.

GEN. We should have gone with the McPhersons. They always have something interesting to say.

BARRY. Not since they went green. If she urges you just once more to use vinegar instead of bleach ... (*HE puts on after-shave.*)

GEN. Are you annoyed I'm taking you?

BARRY. (*Annoyed.*) No.

GEN. Would you like me to slip you a bundle of notes during the meal so you can pretend to pay for me?

BARRY. Flash your credit cards, I don't care.

GEN. Do you ever wish I hadn't qualified?

BARRY. Don't be silly.

GEN. Wish you'd remained the sole breadwinner? You coming home every evening to dinner on the table instead of having a wife earning almost as much as you?

BARRY. Not my fault people started having fewer cavities. And it was a a pity you qualified so late in life.

GEN. Missed the conveyancing gravy train, you mean?

BARRY. Yes. And I wish I'd had someone who paid the bills while I went through university.

GEN. Ooohhh hhoo. I see! Now it comes out!

BARRY. You did change.

GEN. That was the point.

BARRY. I'm trying to be honest, Gen. You asked me, and I said, yes, sometimes I do wish that. Now I'm leapt on for admitting it. I wish it for me, not for you. Life has not been the same since we had separate bank accounts, that's all. It's not worse, just different. There WAS something about pooling everything, call me sentimental—

GEN. How about tight-fisted?

BARRY. Haven't we been over this ground before? Many times?

GEN. Don't resent my enjoying economic independence.

BARRY. I thought the point of nagging was to change present behavior. Not to try and change how a person was in the past.

GEN. Yes. (*Sincere.*) Sorry. Money. When we were students we used to live on next to nothing.

BARRY. Had to save up for a bottle of Spanish plonk. Used to keep it in the fridge.

GEN. (*Puzzled.*) Did we?

BARRY. So we could serve it at room temperature.

GEN. Fool. On the whole, it's been a good twenty-one years.

BARRY. I like to think so.

(*THEY embrace.*)

GEN. I must buy you some better after-shave.

(*PHONE goes.*)

GEN. Hallo. What! I'm sorry. Yes. Right away. (*To Barry.*) Toby's in the Kaufmanns' garden. Got their cat up a tree. And is making a terrible mess of their vegetable garden in the process.

BARRY. Philip! Philip!

GEN. He's at Linda's. You'll have to go.

BARRY. Why me!! You women wanted equal rights,

so you—
   GEN. Because you're dressed!!!!

(Irrefutable. HE goes.)

Scene 3

Later the same evening. Bedroom is empty. The dress we have just seen Gen with is now lying across a chair, plus shoes discarded.
From the bathroom we hear GEN singing ...

GEN.
Once I had a secret love ...
something something ...

(SHE comes in wearing night gown. Checks herself in the mirror. Puts perfume on. Gets into bed. Waits for a moment. Thinks of something. Gets notepad from bedside table. Puts on glasses.)

   GEN. Gillian's trip ... Music exam fee ... Take casserole out of freezer. Collect Philip's shoes. *(Relaxes. Then thinks of something else.)* Dry cleaning ... Tumbleweed. *(Puts LIGHTS off ... lies there. Wistful.)* The Nomadic Tribes ... *(Hears Barry coming towards room. SHE plumps the pillows. Looks very attractive.)*
   BARRY. *(Enters [maybe wearing old dressing gown], carrying a plate of sandwiches. Sees the way Gen is.)* Ah.
   GEN. Barry!

BARRY. I said that place never gives you enough to eat.
GEN. Well ... it's cheese and pickle ... or me. I advise you to choose carefully.
BARRY. Right. Yes. Er ... am I allowed them afterwards ...? Or should I put a bit of cling film over them?
GEN. I'll put cling film over you ...

(HE puts down sandwiches, takes off dressing gown.)

GEN. Talk to me.
BARRY. I thought that's what women say afterwards.
GEN. I've given up hoping for that.
BARRY. Anyway, we've been talking all evening.
GEN. I don't call grumbling about choosing the wrong main course talking.
BARRY. I always manage to do it!
GEN. Tonight ... like old times.
BARRY. Better. You paid. Lights off?
GEN. Not necessarily.
BARRY. I see. (*HE gets into bed. Snuggles up to her.*)
GEN. (*Screams.*) Cold hands!!
BARRY. I know!
GEN. Sod.
BARRY. I know.

(THEY embrace.
During the next sequence, what they say are their thoughts.
  Rather than trying to simulate sexual intercourse, THEY lie quite still. The LIGHTS are dimmed a bit until right at the end.)

BARRY. Should have had those cheese sandwiches downstairs ...

GEN. Should make a hair appointment ...

BARRY. Get into trouble if I don't make some effort.

GEN. Better not put it on the list right now.

BARRY. Tch. Not a flicker down there.

GEN. I wish he'd take his pyjama trousers off.

BARRY. At times like this, is it unfaithful to think of someone else? ... Marilyn Monroe ... Raquel Welch!! No ... no.

GEN. The curtains have got mould!

BARRY. Sandra! My first dental nurse, no second, married, nothing happened worse luck, but sometimes I think she looked at me as if ...

GEN. That mould's quite extensive.

BARRY. Didn't wear a bra. Drove me crazy. I used to think of having her in the surgery ... Last patient would leave and I could say "Now Sandra, I think it's time we ..." Hallo ... torpedo ready for firing. Should have got my pyjama trousers off sooner ...

GEN. He never learns.

BARRY. That's better.

(The next two lines are said together.)

GEN. No he'll put his hand on ...

BARRY. I'll put my hand on ... I know she likes that.

GEN. I once read if all else fails, think of Paul Newman...

BARRY. Come on, come on, I don't want to do this all night ...

GEN. But I wonder who Joanne Woodward thinks of ... Ah, ah, that's nice ...

BARRY. Down in the forest something stirred ...

GEN. Ah! Now we're cooking with gas.

BARRY. Lovely, great, the excitement is mounting. Deliberate pun.

GEN. Nice.

BARRY. Ohhhh lovely.

GEN. Lovely.

BARRY. Lovely.

GEN. Sometimes you wish this could go on for ever.

BARRY. This is what it's all about.

GEN. Mmmmmmmmmmmm.

BARRY. This'd be the way to die.

GEN. (*Almost surprised at herself.*) God this is getting close.

BARRY. Hell's teeth, almost lost it.

GEN. He better hang on or I'll have something to say.

BARRY. Jeepers I better hang on ... whoa whoa ... seven nines are sixty-three ... eight fours are twenty ei— thirty-two—erm come on woman, come on!

GEN. It's so close ...

BARRY. The square on the hypotenuse is equal to the square on the other two ... er, er ...(*Trying to remember.*) come on woman, come on!"

GEN. Ah yes! Yes yes!

BARRY. This is it, the best moment, point of no return, any sec now can't go back, ohhhhhhhh God.

GEN. Yes!

BARRY. OH GOD!! I forgot to pay my VAT!!!!!!

(LIGHTS up quickly.)

GEN. What?
BARRY It was due yesterday. VAT! I forgot to pay it.
GEN. I paid mine.
BARRY. Why didn't you remind me!
GEN. I thought you knew.
BARRY. Damn.
GEN. Oh, very romantic Barry. Thinking of tax at a time like this.
BARRY. It was only afterwards! A good climax clears the mind wonderfully.
GEN. Well, keep your thoughts to yourself another time.
BARRY. You could have said something! I'll have to pay a penalty now.
GEN. Come on, Barry, there's nothing you can do about it now. Give us a cuddle.
BARRY. No.
GEN. Come on.
BARRY. No. Just for that, I'm going to have those sandwiches. (*HE reaches for them.*)

BLACKOUT

Scene 4

Monday evening a week later.
BARRY is at the desk. HE is writing. HE reads out what he has written.

BARRY. The appeal for funds to bring up to date the school's language laboratory is ... "commendable?" ... "worthy of support?" We commend the appeal ... we commend the Old Boys' appeal—(*HE checks his watch—perhaps the alarm has rung.*) Ooh! (*HE sits on the bed and switches on the TV with the remote control. SOUND indicates it's a mid-evening program or some major sporting event. PHONE goes. HE puts TV onto mute.*) Leo! No, I couldn't make it this lunch time. Weren't you? Sorry to hear that. Old age, that's what it is. Happens to us all! Yes. OK, well hope you'll feel better soon. Bye (*HE resumes watching the TV. Hears DOOR. Turns off TV, goes to desk. Pretends to be doing the bills.*)

GEN. (*Enters, from work tired.*) Sorry I'm late. (*Feels the TV, realizes it's warm, and smiles at Barry to show he hasn't fooled her.*)

(*HE gives her some messages. SHE screws one up, puts one in her brief case.*)

GEN. (*Yawns.*) Long hot bath and an early night ...

BARRY. Better go easy on the hot water. Philip's just been in the shower twenty minutes.

GEN. Right.

BARRY. He tells me he intends to sail round the world. Met some guy in the pub who needs another crew member.

GEN. On whose money?

BARRY. Precisely! We had another blazing row as a result. Just the way to meet the sort of trustworthy person to sail round the world with—in a pub. I told Philip any guy that asks him on board for a trip on the Serpentine let alone round the world must be a nutcase.

GEN. Very tactful Barry. Beautifully handled.

BARRY. Threatened to give up university. Leave home. Fine by me, I said. I'll give you a lift to wherever you want to go.

GEN. Barry!

BARRY. Oh! Something else you should know. The party Gillian was at Saturday. Sounded a bit hair raising. Not that it bothered her.

GEN. Gate crashers?

BARRY. Booze.

GEN. I thought the parents were supposed to be there.

BARRY. They were! Anyway, I've said to her if there are any circumstances when she needs our help she can ring us. I've given her a code.

GEN. A code?

BARRY. Sometimes it can be awkward for them to ring up and ask to be collected. If she rings up and says "Did you hear about the Prime Minister?" that means we're to come and get her pronto.

GEN. OK. Anything else? Any other crises?

BARRY. (*Hurt.*) What?

GEN. It'd be nice to come home and not be greeted with details of what the kids are doing wrong.

BARRY. Who used to greet me for years at the door with "Philip scribbled on the wallpaper; Gillian vomited all over the Doctor's waiting room"!!

GEN. That was when I'd been stuck with them all day! We're past all that. (*GEN goes towards the bathroom.*)

BARRY. I took your father shopping.

GEN. Oh. (*Pause.*) Thanks.

BARRY. I had to pay for his groceries.

GEN. Oh no!

BARRY. Mmm.

GEN. I thought he'd stopped all that.

BARRY. I know you did.

GEN. What about the bills? Has he paid them? Rent and power?

BARRY. (*Shrugs.*) Gen. It's time we thought about a home for him.

GEN. A home? He'd hate it.

BARRY. Gen, his place stinks. He stinks. He's got hardly any change of clothes; he wears the same things day after day. He won't spend a penny on buying anything new.

GEN. I have tried.

BARRY. He won't feed himself properly. He's taking pills that have been there for years. He says he can't read the labels.

GEN. He can read the names of horses in the paper! (*Pause.*) What about the Truscott Home? It's nice and it's nearby.

BARRY. There's a waiting list a mile long!

GEN. Isn't one of your old boys on the Board?

BARRY. Oh great! You didn't want my mother here. But when it's one of your parents, that's a different story.

GEN. If your mother had been here, I'd never have been allowed into the kitchen.

BARRY. I thought that was what you wanted.

GEN. Last time she tried to help, she dropped that crystal bowl we got for a wedding present.

BARRY. Women always remember who broke things.

GEN. And the toaster's not the same since your father used it.

BARRY. Gen, he's been dead four years! Your father causes enough tension in this family living where he does now. Have him here, we'd be at each other's throats.

GEN. You're right. It'd be terrible. Damn it! Why can't he stop!

BARRY. Because he doesn't want to!

GEN. You were lucky: You didn't have to go through all this.

BARRY. Thanks. They just died in hospital.

GEN. You know what I mean. It's one thing deciding he should go into a home; but how are we going to persuade him he has to?

BARRY. Simple. We hit him over the head, stuff him in a sack and bingo, he wakes up in the middle of community singing.

GEN. This weekend: We'll start looking at nursing homes. (*Sighs.*) God, it's depressing. (*SHE heads for the bathroom.*)

BARRY. I'd like the water after you. So don't cut your wrists.

GEN. I'm shaving my legs.

BARRY. Great.

Scene 5

Middle of the night.
GEN half asleep in bed.
Sound of loo FLUSHING.

BARRY. (*Comes in from the bathroom.*) No, only the

second time tonight. (*Gets something from wardrobe drawer.*)

    GEN. GRUNTS (What is it now?!)
    BARRY. Cold feet.
    GEN. GRUNTS
    BARRY. Socks.
    GEN. Get to bed.
    BARRY. Can't ... Socks. Can't get them ...
    GEN. GRUNT
    BARRY. Can't get socks ... on. (*Gives up trying to put socks on and gets back to bed.*)

(*DOORBELL rings.*)

    BARRY. Oh no.
    GEN. MUMBLES
    BARRY. Two forty-five. Who on earth could it be? (*Gets dressing gown on. Picks up torch and tests its possibilities as a truncheon. Gets a marine warning device and tests it briefly. Exits.*)

(*GEN sits up listening.
Murmur of VOICES.
BARRY hushing ...
GEN switches on the LIGHT.*)

    BARRY. (*Enters.*) Philip.
    GEN. At this time of night!!
    BARRY. Rather the worse for drink.
    GEN. Oh no.
    BARRY. Steve dropped him off.
    GEN. I thought he took your car?

BARRY. He had the sense not to drive it home. (*Sighs.*) I don't know. He said he and Steve are applying for a fast food franchise ...

GEN. As well as sailing round the world?

BARRY. If he wants money why doesn't he do the jobs we pay him for! He's supposed to mow the lawn; he never does it. Or if he does it looks like a Mohawk haircut. What did we do wrong, Gen?

GEN. I expect you were the same at his age.

BARRY. I was not! At his age, I was failing Medical Part One.

GEN. But WHY did you fail?

BARRY. Ah. Too much rugger, I think. And the pub.

GEN. You came right.

BARRY. Eventually.

GEN. So. Philip'll turn out all right.

BARRY. In our lifetime? Sometimes I think there's no point in saying anything to him. In the end, he'll do what he wants.

GEN. You have to let them know what you think is right. They may not admit it to your face, but it often does have an effect.

BARRY. (*Sighs.*) What's the best thing for Philip right now? A pat on the back or a kick up the bum? It's been like that from early childhood—for both of them. Are we too hard or too soft?

GEN. We'll never know. There's no way you can measure it.

BARRY. Tonight: Should I have stormed at Philip and say he can never have the car again?

GEN. What did you do?

BARRY. Gave him credit for leaving it. Hell, I forgot

to ask him where he left it.
GEN. Probably the right thing.
BARRY. But how do you get him to do his university work!!!
GEN. In the end he's got to do it for himself.
BARRY. I suppose.
GEN. You're too soft on Gillian.
BARRY. Is that right.
GEN. She can be very deceitful.
BARRY. Is she?
GEN. I wish she wasn't friends with Sharon and Rita. Don't trust them an inch.
BARRY. Oh?
GEN. Boy crazy.
BARRY. Great, Gen. Just what I need to be told at three in the morning!

BLACKOUT

Scene 6

Next morning.
BARRY in bed asleep. Gen's side empty.
Radio ALARM starts. BARRY's hand turns it off.
GEN comes out of bathroom from having a shower ...

GEN. Seven forty-five, Barry.

(SHE puts on radio. HE turns it off.)

GEN. (*Goes to the door.*) Philip!! Gillian!!

(*BARRY puts one foot out of the bed and puts it on the floor. HE groans pitifully.*
GEN goes out.)

BARRY. (*Continues slowly to get up. HE focuses on the floor.*) No wonder I couldn't get those socks on! They were gloves! (*Goes to his wardrobe. HE checks underpants. Decides to reject boxer pants and put on Y fronts. HE takes out a singlet. [undershirt] Thinks about it. With reckless abandon HE decides not to wear one. HE goes through to bathroom.*
Sound of electric SHAVER.)

GEN. (*Enters.*) Do you want sandwiches for lunch?
BARRY. Ermmmmm.
GEN. Gillian's making it now.
BARRY. Ermmmmm.
GEN. No, then?
BARRY. Yes.
GEN. (*As SHE goes out.*) Yes he does!!!

(*BARRY scuttles to his brief case. Removes sandwiches from his brief case. Thinks about putting them into waste paper basket. Opens a desk drawer. Finds another lot of sandwiches there. Puts both lots back into brief case.*
GEN enters.
THEY finish dressing.
THEY also make the bed, which BARRY hates doing, and

HE shows his back pain while he does it.)

GEN. Gillian needs a check for £85.
BARRY. What!
GEN. Deposit. The school trip to Innsbruck.
BARRY. Innsbruck!
GEN. Skiing.
BARRY. Skiing! This is the first I've heard of it. Why didn't the school send a note!
GEN. They did.
BARRY. Innsbruck. When I was at school all we got was a trip to the Lake District. Youth hostelling. Trudging through the rain all day and sniggering in the dormitories all night.
GEN. We went to Amsterdam.
BARRY. Follow-up work for the next three weeks.
GEN. I think it's a good idea. Go while they can. £85.
BARRY. Why my account?
GEN. Just write it.
BARRY. I'll write it. Give us your check book.
GEN. What?
BARRY. Ah ah, different story then, isn't it.
GEN. Which reminds me. You still owe me £220 for the dishwasher.
BARRY. Oh God.
GEN. We agreed.
BARRY. It never used to be this way. We used to have a joint account.
GEN. Yes.
BARRY. I put it in; you took it out.
GEN. At least I can go ahead and buy something without consulting you.

BARRY. You always did.

GEN. I'm not going back to the old system.

BARRY. Under the old system, as you call it, we only had a row when we bought something. Now we row about buying things then row trying to work out what we owe each other. I can't see the advantage.

GEN. I never thought you would, Barry.

(HE puts on after-shave.)

GEN. (*Sniffing.*) For anyone in particular?

BARRY. For the people who keep giving me the stuff. How else can I use it up? (*HE reveals three different bottles of it.*)

GEN. (*Starts picking things up off the floor and tidying.*) Mrs. Harlow's coming.

BARRY. Why do we only tidy up when the cleaning lady's coming?

GEN. (*Tidies up some papers that are on the desk.*) Where do you want these? Old Boys' stuff. (*Reads some of them.*) Minutes of meetings.

(BARRY almost snatches them off her and puts them in one of the desk drawers.)

GEN. Tonight? Your fund-raising dinner?

BARRY. Next week.

GEN. What time are you home tonight?

BARRY. Ermmmmm.

GEN. I need to know.

BARRY. Ermmmmm. Yes. Home for tea.

GEN. Good. You can cook it.

BARRY. (*Tricked.*) Oh no. What?

GEN. Casserole's out of the freezer. Potatoes et cetera. I'll be in seven. Ish. Leave mine out for the microwave. Don't let Philip eat all the yogurt. Make sure Gillian eats a good meal. (*SHE grabs her car keys and is about to go. SHE exits. Off.*) Gillian, if you want a ride, I'm leaving now. Yes, now!

(Front DOOR slam. Peace.)

BARRY. (*Pauses. Listens. Dials a number.*) Me. How about lunch today. I thought the Gardens. Sandwiches. Must go. (*HE starts looking for keys. HE thinks.*) Philip! Philip had it. (*As HE goes out.*) Philip!! Where did you leave the car last night? (*Exits.*)

Scene 7

Evening. A week later.
On stage is a school backpack.
PHONE rings.
GEN enters in dressing gown.

GEN. (*Looks annoyed.*) Hallo! (*Switches on charm.*) Edward! No, no, it's not too late. If it's about the James case, I've—badminton! Love to. I thought you usually partnered Rosemary. Is she? I didn't know that. Oh. Well—Yes. Thank you. No, a competition suits me fine;

adds a bit of spice. Where do we play? *(Giggles.)* I mean badminton!

(BARRY enters wearily in dinner suit, bow tie already off. Slumps onto the bed.)

GEN. *(Quickly.)* We can finalize the details tomorrow. Bye. *(Rings off.)* Someone from work, a partner for a badminton tournament. How was the dinner?
BARRY. Terrible. Speakers were terrible. The food was terrible.
GEN. How much did you raise?
BARRY. About a thousand.
GEN. Hardly worth it, for all that effort.
BARRY. Someone has to do it.
GEN. But it doesn't have to be you.
BARRY. Everyone asked where you were.
GEN. I hope you told them that I had better things to do.
BARRY. I just said you couldn't make it.
GEN. Barry, I've got beyond the stage of trotting along dutifully to these things just because I happen to be your wife.
BARRY. Other wives turned up tonight. Other husbands turned up.
GEN. It's your committee, your outfit, your concern. I have nothing to do with it. Life's too short to go along to these things as an appendage. I don't expect you to come to Zonta do's.
BARRY. Oh well—women's groups make it pretty plain they don't want men to come.
GEN. Not true.

BARRY. That's why they're set up in the first place.

GEN. We have functions where husbands are invited, and you're always welcome at them. The difference is I haven't made a fuss about whether you come or not—

BARRY. You can't be bothered to turn up at an Old Boys' fund-raising dinner, but you expect one of the old boys to get your father in.

GEN. You said it was impossible.

BARRY. I had a word with him. He'll put your father on the waiting list.

GEN. (*Appreciative.*) Thanks, Barry.

BARRY. He may not get in for years. Unless there's an epidemic. Was that Linda's car outside?

GEN. Yes. Philip wants Linda to stay overnight.

BARRY. So?

GEN. In his room, Barry. In his bed.

BARRY. No!

GEN. He made it quite clear that's what he meant.

BARRY. I didn't know he was ... they were ...

GEN. What do you think happens when he stays over at her place?

BARRY. I try not to think about it.

GEN. Letting them stay would be a bad example for Gillian.

BARRY. Yes.

GEN. She'd tell Sharon and Rita—it'd be right round the school.

BARRY. I wouldn't get any sleep.

GEN. Why not?

BARRY. I'd be listening. Lucky sod. Why was I born too early?

GEN. You go and tell him.

BARRY. All right. (*HE picks up one of his bedside books. Starts to read.*)
GEN. Better tackle this. (*The backpack.*)
BARRY. What?
GEN. Gillian hates me touching it. I have to wait until she's asleep.
BARRY. A bit underhand.
GEN. I have to do it.

(*SHE starts taking things out of Gillian's bag. Unwashed T-shirts; shorts, crumpled letters, school work, notices ...*)

GEN. Receipt for the Innsbruck trip. Mufti day ... Ah, you see. We wouldn't've known of this [if I hadn't] Meet the teacher evening!!
BARRY. (*Groans.*) When?
GEN. Last week.
BARRY. That's a stroke of luck.
GEN. Philip. Go and tell him.
BARRY. If you've told him—[there's no need for me to]
GEN. Back me up. Tell him!
BARRY. He's not going to like it.
GEN. We're not in the parent business to be liked, Barry.

(*HE goes.*)

GEN. Uggghhhh. (*SHE drags out a crushed and old packet of sandwiches. SHE finds a couple of letters. Reads them with some disgust.*)

(BARRY comes back.)

GEN. That was quick.
BARRY. I just said "Linda, time to go home."
GEN. And Philip accepted it!
BARRY. Yes. Well, he's going with her, of course. *(Depressed.)* I hate having rows with him. I thought I wouldn't have rows with my son the way my father and I did. I thought it was the teacher in him. In some ways, wouldn't it be better if we did let them stay. At least we know where he is, got some sort of control.
GEN. If he wants to enjoy all the advantages of home, then he has to accept the conditions. Next thing Gillian will want to bring someone home.
BARRY. Oh come on. Gillian's not into that.
GEN. Don't you be too sure. Read those. *(Proffering letters.)*
BARRY. *(Reads them.)* Gill didn't write this?
GEN. Sharon. I would think it's all talk but who knows these days?
BARRY. God, it's depressing isn't it.
GEN. And they're both normal.
BARRY. That's what's depressing.
GEN. You should hear some of the things I hear at work. We're well off!
BARRY. You reckon?
GEN. They're good kids. Most of the time we get on with them; they turn up for meals; they still talk to us, crack jokes with us—
BARRY. *(Taking credit for the jokes.)* That's only to be expected—

GEN. You should hear some of the things I hear at work. We're well off!

BARRY. I suppose. (*HE starts to undress.*)

GEN. Hold on. Gillian didn't take Toby for a walk.

(Pause.)

BARRY. Me!

(GEN doesn't have to say anything.)

BARRY. (*About to leave.*) All I ever pray for is that we're both still alive when they've got teenagers.

Scene 8

Early evening.
BARRY and GEN enter, depressed.

BARRY. Did you see that man wearing a hat? Couldn't have been more than early sixties. I've never seen such angry eyes.

GEN. The old ladies kept saying how lucky they were to be in such "a lovely home." And you knew they hated it.

BARRY. You think he won't?

GEN. I know.

BARRY. It's for the best, Gen. He couldn't go on like that.

GEN. I know. I know.

(HE comforts her.)

GEN. If I ever get like that put a pillow over my head.
BARRY. I was going to say the same.
GEN. And no life support system.
BARRY. Agreed.
GEN. We could put it in writing.
BARRY. Yes. Mind you, if we do I'll never be able to get to sleep.
GEN. What?
BARRY. The slightest hesitation in my breathing and I'll hear the pillow come whistling down ...
GEN. Fool.
BARRY. What do we do with his place?
GEN. Not tonight.
BARRY. We have to make a decision some time.
GEN. Not yet! We'll be taking him drives and things. How would he feel if he sees the place with other people in it! He'll know he's never going to leave the home.
BARRY. True. Just have to keep on paying his rent.
GEN. That's all he has to hold on to. The thought of getting well enough to go back home.
BARRY. That's not going to happen.

(GEN doesn't answer.)

BARRY. What a mess. You accuse me sometimes of looking too far ahead, but look what happens if you don't. He could have saved; he could have thought ahead. Stuck in that bloody awful place. For him "Live for today" meant letting William Hill take the lot.

GEN. Yes. All right.

BARRY. We're the one has to pick up the pieces!

GEN. I know!!

BARRY. Sorry. Look, he'll be fine. He's got everything he needs there.

GEN. Except his independence.

BARRY. Do you ever wonder how we'll end up? We've never discussed it. Never made plans.

GEN. For heavens' sake.

BARRY. Your father never planned ahead.

GEN. The difference between my father and us is that we should have enough money. Unless you do something stupid. Even then, I intend to be provided for.

BARRY. I'm not talking money. Stay in this house? Get somewhere smaller when the kids leave home?

GEN. Probably.

BARRY. You know what frightens me. When the kids leave home and poor old Toby dies—we'll have nothing left to talk about.

GEN. We'll be like your parents. Sniping at each other over the sherry. Quarrelling in Sainsburys. That seemed to be their main interest.

BARRY. At least my parents didn't forget they had Christian names! I promise I won't call you Mother if you don't call me Dad.

GEN. Retirement won't make any difference to you. You watching the Old Boys, playing snooker, on committees, reading, watching television. Exactly the same as now except you won't go to work. And you'll get up later.

BARRY. I can't see you content to potter around the house.

GEN. I'll probably be on a cruise of the Greek Islands with a group of Zonta ladies.

BARRY. Greek Islands?

GEN. Yes.

BARRY. You mean ... without me?

GEN. Not always.

BARRY. But—

GEN. We have different interests—more and more. Fine. But I no longer want to go somewhere or do something just because you want to. There isn't enough time left.

BARRY. I've never made you—

GEN. It'll be the same for you! You and Leo'll want to go off on a golf holiday or a walking holiday. Without "the girls."

BARRY. You're saying you want us to lead more independent lives than we do now?

GEN. That's the picture I have.

BARRY. I thought you already had—

GEN. Look. You and Leo go for a day's walking, right? You still imagine, don't you, coming home and finding a meal waiting.

BARRY. Ye-es.

GEN. All I'm saying, there may be a meal waiting; or there may not.

BARRY. But if you come home from something, I'd have a meal for you.

GEN. Barry, the meal isn't the point!

(Pause.)

BARRY. Well. At least I know where I stand.

GEN. Barry! (He's misinterpreting.)

(HE is silent, quite hurt.)

GEN. Barry.

(HE coughs and gives a small moan—the first symptom of flu. GEN grabs a pillow and puts it over his face for a moment.)

BARRY. What are you doing!
GEN. That cough. Thought it was the end.
BARRY. (*Not amused.*) Is that right?
GEN. It would stand up in court. If I had it in writing.

(SHE puts the pillow over him again.
HE grabs a pillow and whacks her with it.
THEY start fighting with the pillows.
At first it is almost vicious, releasing pent-up feelings. But as THEY tire, THEY realize it becomes ludicrous and THEY start laughing. The fight goes all over the room.
Finally GEN collapses on the bed weak from exertion and laughter.
HE flops down beside her.
THEY are about to kiss.
GEN notices something.)

GEN. What's this? Did you put this here?
BARRY. Not now!
GEN. This note. Under my pillow?
BARRY. Later!
GEN. (*Opens it.*) From Philip. (*Reads it.*) Oh no.

(*Hands it to Barry.*) He must have put it there so I'd only find it last thing at night.

BARRY. "Fed up with study. Giving up varsity and getting a job."

GEN. He won't be told.

BARRY. "Am moving in with Linda. Can't stand this place any longer." (*BARRY screws it up and throws it across the room.*)

(*THEY lie side by side on the bed, staring up at the ceiling not moving.*)

End of Act I

Intermission

ACT II

Scene 1

BARRY is in bed with the flu. Empty Ribena bottle, oranges, tissues. HE is sniffing pathetically. HE tries the TV channels. Nothing he wants to see.
GEN enters with washing, ironed, which SHE puts away.

GEN. Talk to Gillian
BARRY. What?
GEN. She'll listen to you.
BARRY. No she won't.
GEN. She wants to take on a morning paper round.
BARRY. What for?
GEN. More money of course. I'm not keen. Fifth form. It's a big year for her. Getting up at 5:45.
BARRY. Let her.
GEN. It won't be you making sure she's up in time.
BARRY. It's a chance for her to get some work experience. The sorts of after-school jobs we could get have all gone.
GEN. If she gets too tired, I'm stopping her.
BARRY. It might give her some idea about money. I'm sick of being treated as if I'm a cash dispenser.
GEN. Stop giving into her so easily.
BARRY. (*Realizing*.) Start a paper round! She goes to Innsbruck in a couple of weeks!
GEN. She says Rita will do it. So you're saying she can

do it?

BARRY. Let her try it. She'll give it up. (*HE gives a pathetic groan.*) I've finished the Ribena.

GEN. (*Mocking.*) There's a good boy.

BARRY. There was a time when you'd make me a nice glass of lemon and honey.

GEN. More fool me.

BARRY. I'm sick. I need the doctor ...

GEN. You've got the flu, Barry. Sweat it out.

BARRY. Nothing on TV.

GEN. Two days in bed you think the world's come to an end.

BARRY. Come to bed.

GEN. You're not serious!

BARRY. I'm so bored.

GEN. You can't be very sick, if you can think of—

BARRY. Only the top half of me's got flu.

GEN. Well, I'm not allowing my bottom half anywhere near you.

BARRY. Just a cuddle, then.

GEN. I'm not getting in that bed at all tonight. It's bad enough when you're healthy, but last night you were like an asthmatic hippo.

BARRY. Sorry!

GEN. Now Philip's away, I can sleep in his room.

BARRY. Charming. You'll be lucky to find the bed.

GEN. I've done a tidy up.

BARRY. More chance of contamination in there than in here with me.

GEN. I'll risk it. You know when you're sick you often wake up in the night and want to read.

BARRY. (*Conceding.*) Mm.

GEN. I could do with a good night's sleep. (*SHE picks up her brief case and starts to leave.*) Er ... I've said I'll have a dinner party here. For the partners.

BARRY. Eddie Maxwell?

GEN. Among others. And don't call him "Eddie." There's no need for you to be here.

BARRY. Oh, charming.

GEN. Barry, of course you're welcome to be here if you want to. I'm only saying you don't have to be. I can understand if an evening of lawyers is your idea of hell.

BARRY. It will be and I'll be there.

GEN. Fine.

BARRY. Where are you going?

GEN. I've got to work on this. I told you. The James custody case.

BARRY. New one on me.

GEN. I told you. A real mess. Sexual abuse suspected but hard to prove, so the kids could end up with the wrong parent.

BARRY. Unlikely, surely.

GEN. Pressure on judges these days, you can't be sure of anything. Meanwhile those poor kids are being shifted from foster home to foster home. It could drag on for weeks.

BARRY. Suddenly dental decay doesn't seem quite so bad.

GEN. I don't want to lose this one. (*SHE is about to go again.*)

BARRY. Work in here!

GEN. I find it easier without a background of sniffing.

(*PHONE rings.*)

BARRY. (*Very weak.*) Hallo. (*Stronger voice when HE realizes who it is.*) Philip! How are you? Good. I am extremely unwell. Your mother is extremely well, but is being a hard-hearted nurse, preferring at present her *LA Law* mode. What job have you found? Aerobics instructor? (*To Gen.*) He's working as an aerobics instructor.

GEN. I gathered.

BARRY. Of course you can speak to her. (*Hands phone to Gen.*)

GEN. Hi. Yes. Yes ... of course. Anything else? No, I'm not doing their laundry, Philip. (*To Barry.*) Wants to bring all his flat mates' laundry round to do in our machine. (*To phone.*) Yes. Of course. Gladly. I'll copy it out for you. See you later then. Bye. (*Rings off. Grins.*) He wants a recipe. Casserole. Liver and bacon.

BARRY. Liver! He hates liver!

GEN. I know. But he's found out how cheap it is! (*SHE almost dances round the room.*) He's discovered something ... he's discovered a fact of life. One of my children has discovered that food costs money! Whoopdedoo!!!!! Well! I never thought I'd see the day!!!!

BARRY. Come to bed.

GEN. (*Laughs.*) You're incorrigible. (*SHE exits.*)

(*HE is about to try the TV channels again.*
PHONE goes.)

BARRY. (*Very weak.*) Hallo. (*Stronger voice when HE realizes who it is.*) Leo! Thank goodness you've rung. I'm at death's door. Roaring temp, can't breathe. Bored out of my tiny mind ... so I'm glad you rang. How's the world treating you? (*Appalled.*) Oh Jesus, Leo, no! Oh God, that's terrible. Next week. They'll know then. Oh Leo, I don't know what to say. Yes, I do. Most cancer cases in fact recover. Are you in any pain? That's something. Anything I can do? OK. Of course. Thanks for ... you know ... letting me ... (*Rings off. HE sits for a moment, shocked by the news.*)

Scene 2

Late evening.
A week or two later.
Sound of CARS driving off.
BARRY enters, eating a piece of food left over from the dinner. HE tests the bed.

BARRY. Dear God, the electric blanket's not on.

(*GEN comes in furious.*
During the following THEY are getting ready for bed, cleaning teeth etc.)

BARRY. The blanket wasn't—
GEN. Were you deliberately trying to ruin my dinner party!
BARRY. What?
GEN. Your bloody jokes.
BARRY. Here we go. What jokes?
GEN. All sex-oriented. Your definition of sex: "a good read interrupted."

BARRY. I always say th(at)—

GEN. "Sex is marvellous—that proves what a great memory I've got."

BARRY. It was a joke! A self-deprecating joke. Puts guests at their ease.

GEN. It put the hostess on edge. Are you trying to imply to the world that we no longer—

BARRY. No—

GEN. The pulse rate joke!

BARRY. The pulse rate! It's a true story! The doctor told Roy he had to cut down on excitement because of his heart. Roy said "You mean no sex?" and the doctor said "Well, with your wife it's OK because the pulse rate is hardly affected."

GEN. I was there Barry when you told it. I didn't find it funny the first time.

BARRY. Roy swears it's true. I find it very funny.

GEN. I noticed.

BARRY. Maxwell thought it funny.

GEN. Never again. All right?

BARRY. Right.

(Pause.)

BARRY. Jokes or sex?

GEN. Both.

BARRY. I had to do something. He never asks questions, have you noticed that? Your friend Maxwell. You ask him how he is and he tells you! For about twenty minutes. I ask him about his work and he tells me. Does he ask me about my work?

GEN. What is there to tell?

BARRY. Oh God, the law, the law. You all think it's so wonderful you're all up yourselves. If it's so wonderful why do so many lawyers fuck things up.

GEN. What?

BARRY. Look, they're doing well, they're making money, then they get themselves in some crazy scheme to make even more money. Or they deal in dope. Or something.

GEN. Maybe people get sick of things after they've been doing it for twenty-five years.

BARRY. They do. They do. Believe me, they do. But at least I don't dip into someone else's trust funds to finance some harebrained property deal. Just dull old Barry.

GEN. Don't be pathetic.

BARRY. All right! How about my giving up work and you supporting me.

GEN. Oh great. Wait till the children are about to leave and then you want to stay at home.

BARRY. I can just see you setting up on your own. A little flat in the centre of town for the professional woman. Bijou place. Can't move for cushions on the floor.

GEN. It has its attractions, yes.

BARRY. You'd love that on your own, wouldn't you? You would.

GEN. I'd settle for someone with a bladder that lasts the night.

BARRY. Here we go.

GEN. What is it you want Barry?

BARRY. What I don't want is seeing you smarming over a prick like Maxwell just because he's a legal big shot.

GEN. Don't be ridiculous.

BARRY. You do! When you were young you despised people like him. When you first took up law, you were fired up a lot of the time. Angry about this and that. You loved that quote I found for you, remember? "Justice was on his side but the law was against him."

GEN. (*Irritated to be reminded of it.*) Tch!

BARRY. Remember?

GEN. You're not accusing me of selling out.

BARRY. You're not making enough for me to accuse you of that!

GEN. I make as much as you.

BARRY. Maxwell. You think the sun shines out of his briefs.

GEN. He's a damn good lawyer.

BARRY. And he's a bloody awful human being. And women think he's bloody Christmas.

GEN. Not jealous are you?

BARRY. I'm jealous to think that someone like that impresses you! That you can't see through him. Smarm city.

GEN. Just because you .... (*SHE stops.*)

BARRY. Yes? Say it. Just because I haven't grown old that gracefully ... that's what you were going to say, isn't it. No foxy silver mane on my head. No silver-tongued oratory to sway a jury or get the pants off impressionable legalistic bimbos.

GEN. You think he's got my pants off, don't you!

BARRY. It wouldn't surprise me.

(*Silence.*)

BARRY. I take that back. It would surprise me.

GEN. (*SHE gets into bed, turns off her light and lies down.*) One thing I learned tonight. It's obvious I don't excite you any more.

BARRY. I thought it was mutual. Sometimes you come to bed like Mary Queen of Scots approaching the scaffold.

GEN. Yes. Well. Her executioner made a hash of it, too.

(HE is now in bed.)

GEN. If I do happen to be in the mood, I'm rejected in favor of snooker on the telly.

BARRY. That should tell you something, shouldn't it? (*Turns off the light.*) Well, from now on you'll just have to lie back and think of Maxwell.

GEN. I do.

Scene 3

A week later. Daytime.
GEN, wearing dark clothes, enters. Sits on bed.
BARRY comes in a moment later. HE is wearing black tie.

BARRY. They've gone. (*Pause.*) It was a bigger turn out than I expected.

GEN. It seems so final, so quick. A couple of days ago he was alive; now they've scattered his ashes.

BARRY. You did well, Gen. It's not easy.

GEN. He wasn't a very nice man.

BARRY. He was your father.

GEN. He was totally selfish.
BARRY. Plenty worse.

(Silence.)

BARRY. I thought William Hill could have sent a wreath.
GEN. We were all right to him weren't we? Over the last years? We did enough for him?
BARRY. Yes. Yes.
GEN. I should have spent more time with him. I was so busy.
BARRY. He knew that.
GEN. He hated my having a job. We could have had him here. It wouldn't have been for long.
BARRY. We didn't know that. And it wouldn't have worked.
GEN. And the kids should have seen him more ...

(Silence.)

GEN. I never thought Philip would cry. (*SHE cries.*)
BARRY. (*Hugs her.*) I know. I know.
GEN. Do you think we'll be a nuisance to them? To Gill and Philip, when we're old.
BARRY. I certainly intend to be. Got to get some return on our money.
GEN. Fool.
BARRY. I can't imagine Philip taking me for Sunday afternoon drives, but I expect Gillian will. Take me to drool over the ducks.
GEN. That was my mother's greatest fear. "Being a

nuisance" to us.

BARRY. We're the oldest generation, now, you realize that? My parents gone; now yours. Most of the uncles and aunts have popped off.

GEN. Mm.

BARRY. Head of the family stuff. Next thing, it'll be us they'll be putting under.

GEN. It's frightening.

BARRY. Death?

GEN. How quickly it all goes. How many summers have we got left?

BARRY. Who knows?

GEN. There's still so much I want to do.

BARRY. I've never been to Austria ... You realize when Gillian's away we'll have the place to ourselves?

GEN. Mm.

BARRY. It'll be a taste of what it's like when they've both left home.

GEN. Bliss.

BARRY. I doubt it. Even now I sometimes hear you opening Philip's door in the morning to wake him up.

(GEN acknowledges this.)

BARRY. It's like that time in the car, remember? When they were little, and always quarrelled in the back. Drove me crazy! And one day we were going somewhere and I yelled "Be QUIET back there", and the kids weren't even in the car.

(SHE smiles.)

BARRY. (*Stands up.*) Well! You're not going to work this afternoon?

GEN. I'll help Gill and Philip clear up here.

BARRY. I better finish clearing up his flat. Throw away his sweater, all that sort of stuff. Burn his tie. Anything you want?

GEN. No. I took what I wanted the other day. (*Warmly.*) Thanks for doing that. I couldn't bear it.

BARRY. Purely selfish, Gen. I keep thinking I might find a stash of ten pound notes somewhere. (*Sighs.*) Then a nice night in front of the telly. (*Grins.*) Not sport. (*HE starts to leave.*)

(*PHONE goes.*)

GEN. Hallo? Hang on! (*Holds it out to Barry.*)

BARRY. Meeting. Tonight! Yes I had forgotten. The brochure? Er ... it's coming on ... OK, I'll be there. *(Rings off.).* Another bloody Old Boys' meeting. Damn it. I suppose I'll have to go now I've said I would. (*Sighs.*) I'll say this for death—at least it gets you off committees.

Scene 4

Late.
Room in DARKNESS.
BARRY tiptoes in. BARRY peers at the bed.

BARRY. Gen? Gen? (*HE switches on the light.*) For heaven's sake. (*Looks round a bit.*) Where the hell is she?

(Rings a number.) Needn't have worried. The coast was clear. Yes. Very. See you tomorrow. Me too. Night. *(HE starts listening to the messages. Sound of CAR arriving. HE turns off the machine. Front DOOR shut.)*

GEN. *(Enters. Happy with bottle of champagne and two glasses.)* I rang you!

BARRY. I rang you.

GEN. To join us.

BARRY. Where have you been?

GEN. To Orso's. They're making me a partner!

BARRY. A partner.

GEN. Yes.

BARRY. *(Not pleased.)* Fantastic. Wonderful. Terrific.

(SHE pours him a glass and offers it.)

BARRY. No thanks, it gives me headaches. *(HE grabs the phone book. Looks through Yellow Pages.)*

GEN. What are you (doing)?

BARRY. Looking for the Alfa agents. You'll want to trade up from the Uno to an Alfa Romeo, won't you? Oh, and the gold credit card. That's a must.

GEN. You're supposed to be pleased.

BARRY. Thrilled. It would have been nice to have had the chance to celebrate with my wife. Or was it a Law Society exclusive? *(Thinks of something.)* We should ring Gillian! That sort of news can't wait till she gets back. What's the dialing code for Innsbruck?

GEN. I rang! Several times. And left a message. To see if you could join us.

BARRY. Sorry.

GEN. Where were you?

BARRY. Movies. *Indiana Jones and The Last Crusade*.

GEN. You've seen it once!

BARRY. Now I've seen it twice. So ... you obviously had a good time.

GEN. I did. I did.

BARRY. A partnership, eh? Right in the upper income bracket.

GEN. Not for ages. You have to buy into it.

BARRY. Ah but what a little nest egg for your retirement! Totally independent then, won't you. Won't need me at all.

GEN. I was going to save the other piece of news 'til later, but let's get all the unpleasantness over now shall we. They've asked me to go to a Law Conference.

BARRY. Don't tell me. Munich? Milan?

GEN. New York.

BARRY. Same thing. Well! Austria ... the USA—the women are getting around.

GEN. You went to dental conferences!

BARRY. Three. In total.

GEN. This is one.

BARRY. So far.

GEN. It's only seven days Barry. And don't panic. I'll make sure the freezer's full.

BARRY. Don't worry. I'll probably go Orso's each night. Or McDonalds.

GEN. You're being a mean-spirited shit, Barry. When I think back! I had to celebrate your stupid dental degree; attend the stupid dinner, listening to the stupid speeches, and then hang around till dawn for the stupid champagne breakfast!

BARRY. We went to a party to celebrate your law

degree! I seem to remember hearty young men vomiting into the hydrangeas.

GEN. You were sulking because my degree pass was better than yours.

BARRY. Oh rubbish, everyone gets a better pass these days.

GEN. Barry, I made every effort to get you to join us tonight. I did ring you before you would have gone to the movies.

BARRY. Went to see Leo.

GEN. Oh. How was he?

BARRY. The surgeons are very optimistic. He could be out in a week.

GEN. That's wonderful.

BARRY. 'Course I've been a bit of a fool. I thought, both kids away, this was our chance for a second honeymoon.

GEN. Being at home is not a second honeymoon.

BARRY. True. And you haven't even missed them, have you?

GEN. Barry! Gill's away for ten days and she's phoned us twice.

BARRY. Reversed the charges.

GEN. Philips always coming round to borrow things. What has there been to miss? I don't know why I bothered to come home.

BARRY. What?

GEN. Some of them were going on to a nightclub.

BARRY. (*Patronizing*.) They're lads, aren't they? Spending what they've creamed off the latest round of divorces, mm? Or is it property that's the big money spinner these days?

GEN. Anything else?
BARRY. What?
GEN. Anything else to spoil tonight for me?

(Silence.)

BARRY. You're right. I'm sorry, Gen. I apologize. And congratulations on the partnership. You deserve it. (*HE starts to leave.*)
GEN. Where are you going now!
BARRY. Take Toby for a walk. Goodnight. (*HE leaves.*)

Scene 5

A few weeks later. Early morning.
GEN in bed half asleep. SHE has shifted over towards Barry's side, which is empty.
BARRY enters in old clothes. [running gear] HE is in an ebullient mood, virtuous from having stood in for Gillian and getting up early. HE has two cups of tea and several morning papers.

BARRY. Cup of tea! Cup of tea! Cup of tea! (*HE puts them down.*) Shift, shift, shift!

(GEN reluctantly moves back to her side.)

BARRY. (*Gets back into bed.*) Quite enjoyed it. Knocked fourteen minutes off her best time. Toby liked it.

GEN. You're not coming back to bed!

BARRY. Yes. Quite a lot of papers left over. Can't quite work it out.

GEN. You have to get up again in twenty minutes.

BARRY. Twenty minutes is twenty minutes. If Gill's still sick tomorrow, I'll do it again. You'd get fit.

(SHE is struggling to wake up and drink her tea.)

BARRY. Supposed to be a treat, this. Cup of tea and the paper in bed.

GEN. It would be, if I were by myself.

BARRY. British Gas is up five. Nice start to the day for me. Probably all downhill from now on. Let's see ... what sort of day Mrs. G. M. Masefield for the defense will have.

GEN. Barry.

BARRY. Three cases of driving with excess breath alcohol level; two shoplifters.

GEN. Just shut up.

BARRY. But mostly it will be acting for women who have left their husbands and want you to negotiate for all they can get.

GEN. My job.

BARRY. Of course. But how much sweeter when you're united in a common cause against the enemy.

GEN. What enemy?

BARRY. Men.

GEN. Barry. You've been in a foul mood ever since I went to New York.

BARRY. Went Business Class to New York.

GEN. What's bugging you?

BARRY. You're off to fight the good fight. Now what

sort of day am I going to have? Mrs. Childs, two fillings. Harry Stainton, one filling, check gums. Mrs. Giles, six-monthly check up, scale and polish. Only fifteen more years or so of that and I can retire.

GEN. Well do four days a week instead of five, then! Get a partner and only work alternate weeks. We can afford it. But stop whining.

BARRY. Ah no no no. If I did that I might have to dip into your separate account, and we can't have that can we.

GEN. God, you've got so boring, Barry. Absolutely predictable. I don't mind what you do with your working life. If you want to coast along, that's fine by me. But DON'T take it out on me because I want something different from my job!

BARRY. Predictable, am I? Boring?

GEN. Absolutely.

BARRY. I see. "How weary, stale, flat and unprofitable—"

GEN. What is it you want Barry? What have I done? I thought we had everything. You accuse lawyers of messing things up; you're going the right way about it yourself. Decide what you want and do it, but lay off the continual sniping at me!

BARRY. Me! Snipe?

GEN. I'm serious, Barry.

BARRY. And never looked lovelier.

(Furiously SHE gets out of bed. The PHONE rings.)

GEN. Hallo. Yes. My daughter's sick, so my husband delivered the papers for her. Right. I'll tell him. (*Rings off.*)

GEN. Those papers you had left over. You forgot to do

Willoughby Gardens.

(HE leaps out of bed. SHE laughs. BARRY rushes out.)

MUSIC: "Hard Day's Night"

Scene 6

A couple of weeks later. Early evening.
BARRY walking up and down.
GEN enters in a hurry. In badminton outfit. Rummages in her wardrobe for sports shoes. Maybe puts on a track suit.
BARRY is sitting on the bed not talking.

BARRY. Gen.
GEN. I told Gill no later than twelve—the number where she's at is by the downstairs phone.
BARRY. Where—?
GEN. At a party. Parents will be there—I've checked.
BARRY. Gen.
GEN. Playing Skelton Anderson McKay tonight ... arch rivals.
BARRY. Gen.
GEN. If we beat them, we win our section.
BARRY. Gen. We have to talk—
GEN. Half the office coming along to watch.
BARRY. The office, the office, the bloody office!!!!! For Christ's sake think about home for a few minutes.
GEN. I will. When I get back.

BARRY. If I was a message on the answer phone, you'd listen to me.

GEN. Barry, I promise. When I get back, you'll have my divided attention. (*SHE starts to leave then comes back.*) Oh. If we do win, we'll probably celebrate.

BARRY. Don't drink out of someone else's tennis shoe.

(SHE exits.)

BARRY. (*Shouting after her.*) Don't say I didn't try!

(Slam of front DOOR.
BARRY is very angry. HE goes to the desk. Starts to write a note. Tears it up twice.
PHONE goes.)

BARRY. Gillian's not in I'm afraid. She's at a party. Anthea's. Oh, is it? She should be there any sec, she left quite a while ago. OK. (*Rings off. HE makes third attempt on note and is reasonably satisfied. Puts it in an envelope and places it on her side of the bed. Takes a couple of hold-alls out from his wardrobe. They are packed, but HE puts in a couple of extra things, including one book from his bedside reading. Dials a number.*) Me. Just leaving. No ... I tried ... it would have spoiled her pre-match build-up. If she lost her match because I told her I was leaving she'd never have forgiven me. Joke. So I've been told. (*Irritated.*) This end is my problem, all right! I have a million doubts, but then I do even when I'm choosing a ball-point pen, so ... Be there soon. Bye. (*Rings off. HE puts on an overcoat. Picks up cases. PHONE rings. HE looks at it. Walks out. Comes back to answer it.)* Gillian! Anthea rang for you, did she say? Having a good time? I didn't hear about the Prime Minister, no. There was nothing on the news about the Prime Min—*(Realizes.)* Shit! Right. Where are you? What are you doing th(ere)—I'll be right over. *(HE leaves in a hurry. Comes back still holding cases. Puts them down. Dials a number.)* Me. Family emergency. I have to get Gillian urgently so I can't make it tonight. Look ...when it actually comes down to it, I don't think I can go through with this. Carry on as we are, yes, but not ... No. I'm sorry. Can we meet to talk it—*(She has rung off. BARRY sits for a moment, then realizes he has to rush. Exits.)*

Scene 7

Later that night.
GEN is sitting at the desk still in her track suit.

BARRY. *(Enters, excited, holding a large drink.)* Boy, do I need this. Do you realize Gillian WASN'T at the party you said she was? She and Sharon and Rita had arranged to meet and go to this other one. You should have seen it! Motor bikes outside. The hall full of yobs, bikers. There were two Rotweilers. I was terrified. Took me ages to get in, to start with. Thought I was a cop, probably. I just said I've come for my daughter. I got pushed in the chest, I really thought I was going to get done over. And once I did get in, I couldn't find her. Pot everywhere, lots of other stuff. The nightmare that kept running through my head was I'd find her in a bedroom, being raped. And what could I do about it. It was really scary. And a lot of them were so hostile ! I thought I was going to make it worse for her. I found her and her friends bailed up in one of the rooms by some skinheads. They were not pleased to see me. Anyhow, got them all out. Her friends made me swear not to tell their parents. Gillian was very frightened. She's learned her lesson. I think she's realized now why we take all these precautions about where she is at parties. I need another drink. (*HE is about to go.*)

GEN. You're supposed to cross your bridges before you burn them.

BARRY. Mm?

GEN. Your note. (*SHE waves it at him.*)

BARRY. Oh God! I forgot. Christ. That's all cancelled. Wiped. Forget it.

GEN. I can hardly do that.

BARRY. I'm not going now.

GEN. Want to bet?

BARRY. Well, I'm not.

GEN. Is this how you were going to tell me. A note!!!

BARRY. If you recall, I was trying to tell you before you went off to Centre Court Wimbledon, but you were so excited at the prospect of flashing your knickers in front of the partners—Sorry, the OTHER partners.

GEN. It could have waited!!

BARRY. No. If you're on the high diving board and you don't go straight away, that's it. You lost the badminton, I take it, or else you'd still be there quaffing on the business account.

GEN. Lost.

BARRY. And then come home to a "Dear Gen" letter.

Not your night.

GEN. It still could be. Who's the lucky lady?

BARRY. Forget it.

GEN. Stop suggesting I have a bad memory.

BARRY. No one you know. A patient. Never thought anything about her. One day she made a joke. I mean I make jokes all the time, relax the patients, all that. But it's rare to have anyone make one back at me. Usually they can't, of course, mouth full of novocaine ... Anyway, I said how about lunch?

GEN. It always starts with "How about lunch?"

BARRY. If you know so much about it, why ask? It's been someone else to talk to, Gen. Tell things to. It's like being given another life. Anyhow, I'm not going and that's that.

GEN. So that's it, is it. All behind you?

BARRY. I couldn't do it. Couldn't abandon the family.

GEN. I should have said something much sooner. I thought it would just die a natural death.

BARRY. You knew?

GEN. Of course. I knew there was someone.

BARRY. How?

GEN. When you go to monthly Old Boys' meetings once a fortnight. Especially when you leave the minutes around and they've recorded your apologies. Anyway I knew before that.

BARRY. How?

GEN. You started driving faster and stopped wearing vests. Did you ever bring her here?

BARRY. Of course not, you know how much I hate making the bed.

(GEN doesn't laugh.)

BARRY. It was meant to be a joke.
GEN. Yes, I did recognize the form.
BARRY. Anyway ... I thought you and Maxwell ...
GEN. Yes?
BARRY. Were ...

(Pause.)

GEN. Yes?

(Silence.)

GEN. No. At least, not until ...
BARRY. New York?

(Silence.)

BARRY. I thought so. Him! God, Gen what do you see in him? Apart from his being good looking and enormously successful?
GEN. He doesn't make jokes at the wrong time.
BARRY. Really? Not even when you take your bra off?
GEN. There you go again!!
BARRY. Of course he doesn't make jokes at the wrong time. He doesn't make jokes at all. Humour implies a sense of proportion; he has none. His is an entirely egocentric world.
GEN. Anyway, it's all finished. Not that it amounted to anything. And if it's any consolation, I feel sick about it. With myself.

BARRY. Self-induced nausea washes away the sin, does it? Do I get the chance to ask you how it happened? Or shall we just call it quits.

GEN. We will not call it quits!!

BARRY. Why ever—(not)!!

GEN. You were going to leave! Going to leave me!

BARRY. What?

GEN. You only stayed because of Gillian. Not because of me. If Gillian hadn't phoned for Daddy to come to the rescue, you'd be there now, cracking jokes and forgetting your back pain.

BARRY. I'm not, am I. When it came down to it, I remained.

GEN. It's not me you're staying for. That's the whole point.

BARRY. Weren't you ever tempted to live with him in his penthouse? Or isn't his kitchen as nice as ours!

GEN. I was never going to leave. Never.

BARRY. That's what everyone thinks. At first. And you getting shrill about being left behind. Your scenario for retirement didn't exactly make me feel wanted.

GEN. Oh so that's why you wanted to go to her. To come home from walking to a nice roast.

BARRY. The only reason you'll want me around in old age is to halve the gas bill.

GEN. Don't exaggerate.

BARRY. I was tempted to go because we've got interests in common. We can talk about things.

GEN. That sounds so adolescent.

BARRY. Not as adolescent as "I feel sick with myself." I'm glad you managed to find the higher moral ground, Gen. Enjoy the view.

(HE gets his pyjamas and a book from the hold-all he'd packed.)

BARRY. I'm shifting into the next room.

(Front DOORBELL rings.)

BARRY. Who the hell can that be at this time of night!
GEN. I'd think it's very probably your jilted lady friend. Wouldn't you.
BARRY. Jesus. *(HE exits.)*

(GEN takes the cases and throws them out of the room; takes his bedside reading and does the same.)

BARRY. *(Enters.)* Philip. He's come back. To live.

Scene 8

Evening. A few days later.
GEN is at the desk, working.
BARRY enters. Not very pleased to see her there. HE sees a note on his side of the bed.

BARRY. Yes, I'll pick Gillian up from her music exam tomorrow. And do the shopping. Ah! My washing's out of the machine. Oh, bliss. Gen, I need to borrow your car. Philip's got mine and I need to go back to the surgery.

(SHE throws her car keys onto the bed.)

BARRY. We have to talk some time.

*(No response.
PHONE rings.)*

BARRY. Philip's not in, Linda. He says he's at the university library—that's what he's got my car for.

(GEN, irritated by the distraction, goes out.)

BARRY. I'll get him to ring when he gets back home. Linda, we appreciate what you did—encouraging him to go back. He does seem to be trying hard to catch up, but without you ... (he would never have done so). Thanks. We'll see you around. Bye.

*(GEN enters with her washing, neatly ironed and stacked. BARRY exits.
GEN puts her washing away and then resumes work at the desk.
BARRY enters with his washing in basket. It is all creased and unsorted. HE stuffs it away in drawers and in his wardrobe. HE is left with one spare sock, which HE finds very puzzling. HE goes to ask Gen, but can't. HE puts the sock on one hand and uses it as a glove puppet. HE folds his arms so that the sock appears over the ledge formed by the other arm.)*

BARRY. I used to do this for the kids. Hallo, what's your name? *(Puts on funny voice.)* "My name is Sammy

Sock." Well, Sammy, your partner is missing. "My partner. Samantha? Missing?" I'm afraid so. "Do something about it." What? "Ask." I daren't—I'm still in the dog box. "Then I will." No, no, you mustn't. (*BARRY aims the sock towards Gen.*) "Where is Samantha Sock?"

(*No reply.*)

BARRY. (*Even more deliberate.*) "Where is my partner, Sam—"

(*GEN wheels round in fury.*
BARRY makes the sock hide as if in fear.
GEN picks up her work and is about to storm out.
BARRY leaps up and bars her way.)

BARRY. This is impossible Gen. We cannot carry on like this.

(*Silence.*)

BARRY. Grovelling apology? You've got it. Written permission to sleep with Maxwell? Here. Force worse conditions on me than Germany had to accept after World War One if you want. But damned if I'm going to have to tip toe and be mute in my own room.

(*Silence.*)

BARRY. If some woman phoned up right now in distress, you'd talk to her. But me, your own husband!

(Silence.)

BARRY. Gen. We have to talk.
GEN. All right.
BARRY. Well? Do you want to go? Do you want me to go?

(Silence.)

BARRY. Stay together?
GEN. Can we really face each other for another twenty, thirty years?

(Silence.)

GEN. I don't know why you're staying. In these situations the man nearly always wins out financially and the woman ends up worse off.
BARRY. Not in our case. You'd get old Egocentric Eddie Maxwell to represent you. He'll be happy to screw me as well.

(Pause.)

GEN. I'll outline for you the way it goes. The break-up starts off in a reasonably civilized fashion. Things will be split down the middle. Ah, but then who gets the paintings? Who did, in fact, decide to buy the antique carriage clock? Later, it's who pays for the teeth, the music lessons, the school skiing trip...? Continual guerilla warfare, Barry. And the children. Oh they're mature teenagers, they can handle the world. We've got them through those difficult years. Rubbish. It'll affect them all right. And we'll use them as spies. Did he have anyone with him? Who was she? What has she been buying lately? Then there's revisionist history: things done or said ten years ago are seen in a new light. Ah! I thought at the time it meant such and such whereas NOW I realize it actually meant something quite different. It's one long miserable mess, Barry.

BARRY. Agreed. Is this what you want?

GEN. It's what YOU wanted!

BARRY. No—

GEN. You were prepared to inflict it on us all. You were walking out. You'd packed your bags.

BARRY. But in the end I didn't. When it came to it, I couldn't.

GEN. We'll never know whether it was sense of duty or lack of balls.

BARRY. It doesn't occur to you that it might take more balls to live with you.

GEN. Because you can't hack my having a career? Because I'll be earning more than you?

BARRY. You enjoy it, Gen. You enjoy staying behind working, drinks with the chaps, flying business class ... It'll all be spending money for you. I've provided the house, the car, the Turkish rugs ... once that's all in place you come along, scoop up all that lovely money and stash it into your separate account. Me. I think I'll go walking ...

GEN. Well! Are you happy now? Now that I've broken my vow of silence, has that "cleared the air?" "Made things better?" "Channels of communication re-established?"

BARRY. You still haven't made it clear whether it's to

be war or peace.

GEN. Truce, Barry. War could be resumed at any moment.

Scene 9

Evening. Some weeks later.
BARRY is at desk. HE writes something. Crosses it out.
   Writes again.

BARRY. In these days of economic union, languages will be increasingly important. That's why we're asking You, as an Old Boy, to contribute ... "to give"? ... "to pledge"! ... to pledge so much a month ... "a quarter"? Where's that brochure Rotary put out for the sports centre...? (*HE searches in the desk drawers ... a mess. Reaches right back into one drawer ... HE pulls an old notebook out of the drawer.*) So that's where it was! (*HE flicks through it. Reads one of two entries.*) Ah yes! "Justice was on his side, but the law was against him." Thomas Love Peacock!

"The mass of men lead lives of quiet desperation." Yes, yes yes, very familiar.

   "I wish I were a little grub
   With hairs around my tummy.
   I'd jump into a honey pot
   And make my tummy gummy."

Very edifying. (*Trying to remember.*) There was one I was going to add ... Ah yes. "If you are afraid of loneliness, don't marry." Chekhov. (*Before he actually writes in it, HE notices another piece. Reads it to himself. Is moved by it. PHONE goes. HE is re-reading the piece to himself as HE goes to the phone, and then marks that place. HE leaves the notebook on the bed.*) Hallo. She's not in yet, she shouldn't be much longer. Can I...? Yes. Yes ... could you repeat that? Yes. I'll tell her. (*HE stares at the message he's written down for a moment or two.*)

GEN. (*Enters. SHE is very upset.*) What a mess, what a mess, what a rotten miserable mess! We lost the case. We lost!

(*BARRY tries to take hold of her to comfort her. SHE shakes him off.*)

GEN. The judge must have been blind!
BARRY. What case—?
GEN. The James custody case!
BARRY. I'll get you a drink?
GEN. Yes. No! I've already had some. He said that in his opinion because the children had been shifted from home to home that above all they must be given a stable secure home.
BARRY. Sounds reasonable.
GEN. He gave them to the wrong parent! Who'd caused all the mess in the first place.
BARRY. Oh God. Here we go. Another zealous man-hating social worker wants to deprive some poor bugger of his kids because she's fired up by a lot of spurious statistics, and you happen to strike a judge who can see through all that—
GEN. We represented the father, Barry!
BARRY. But—

GEN. The father should have got them. Now they're back with her!

BARRY. Didn't you once say something about sexual abuse?

GEN. She was the one suspected of abusing them. But it's almost impossible to prove. The guy is devastated. (*In tears.*) I would be, too ...

(*Again HE tries to comfort her. SHE shakes him off.*)

GEN. We worked so hard on that case. A decent, hard-working guy trying to do the right thing; and he has to see her walk away with them. He'll hardly ever get to see them again ...

(*Pause.*)

GEN. What could I say to him Barry?

(*BARRY shakes his head; HE has no answers.*)

GEN. It makes you want to throw it all in.
BARRY. Don't do that.
GEN. You win cases for people who you'd be doing everyone a favor if they were put away; and you lose ones that really count.
BARRY. When my father started teaching someone said to him "If you don't have days when you think 'I should never have been a teacher'—then you shouldn't be a teacher." I'm sure it applies equally to the Law.
GEN. I thought that's what you wanted me to do. Chuck it in.

BARRY. Whatever gave you that idea? Just because I slag off at you and lawyers all the time. No, no, no. Just my little way. Let me get you a drink. Large scotch? Brandy? Pint of Drambuie? Tea? Coffee? Horlicks? Run you a Badedas bath. Give you a foot massage, neck massage, whisper naughty things into your shell-like. You know something, play your cards right, you could have me tonight.

GEN. (*Has begun to relax.*) From that menu I'll take the bath and the large scotch.

BARRY. Will there be anything else, Madam?

(SHE smiles but shakes her head.)

BARRY. Ah, well. God loves a trier. (*Starts to go to the bathroom. HE hesitates.*) Er ... a Wendy Hammersley wants you to ring back. Fairly urgent.

GEN. (*Angry.*) I told her not to—(ring here)! (*SHE stops.*)

BARRY. "A flat that's just come onto the market."

(GEN doesn't answer.)

BARRY. Are you planning to...?

GEN. I'm just looking. For a flat. In town. I don't want to live in it. An investment. It would be nice to have ... when we retire. Maybe a place in the Algarve ... and a place in town. It makes sense.

BARRY. But you weren't going to tell me?

GEN. (*Facing up to it.*) And I wanted a place as a bolt hole. If things go wrong ... here ... I know it's there. If I need it. A place I've chosen. And furnished and decorated myself.

BARRY. I guess I deserve it.

GEN. I can't stand much more of the way we've been living lately, Barry.

BARRY. Fair enough.

GEN. I've got a career and I intend to do well at it. You have to face it.

BARRY. I have faced it! Not well. Badly. But I have come to terms with it.

GEN. Grudging acceptance isn't enough, Barry. I need you to support me.

BARRY. One concession at a time, Gen! Don't push your luck. I'm still getting used to being bedfellows with a legal partner; it's a little early in the day to expect me to become an arse-licking worshipper.

GEN. You're impossible. You never let up.

BARRY. Impossible, no. Difficult, yes. For the defense, I would point out that a) I have apologized, b) I have adjusted to your new-found elevated status, and c) I thought one got time off for good behavior. I shall go and run a bath for the prosecution. (*HE starts for the bathroom. Stops.*) Ring her. Ring Wendy Whatsit, buy the flat and order the scatter cushions.

GEN. If that's what you think's for the best.

(*HE doesn't answer.
SHE turns to the phone. It RINGS.*)

GEN. Hallo. Yes. (*SHE hands it to Barry.*)
BARRY. (*Angrily.*) Yes!
BARRY. Pam. Oh no. When? That's awful. I'm sorry. If there's anyt— Yes. Yes, of course. Thanks for lett—

(*Rings off.*)

BARRY. Leo's dead. Died early this evening. Fifty-one. (*HE lets out a howl of pain.*) Fifty-one. (*HE weeps.*)

GEN. (*Comforts him.*) Barry.

BARRY. Fifty-one.

GEN. Barry.

BARRY. As decent, fine, gentle a man as you're ever likely to find.

GEN. Barry.

BARRY. Ah, God. I am impossible.

GEN. It's all right. It's all right.

BARRY. I don't know what makes me—

GEN. Shush. Here.

(*THEY are lying on the bed. SHE comforts him.*)

BARRY. How long have we got left? How long have any of us got left?

GEN. I know, I know.

BARRY. I said I'd run you a bath.

GEN. It can wait ... What's this?

(*BARRY has almost forgotten he left it there.*)

BARRY. Oh that. My old quotes notebook. I thought this apt ... it's Milton. Eve to Adam after the Fall: (*HE hands it to her.*)

GEN.
> "While yet we live
> Scarce one short hour perhaps, between us two
> Let there be peace."

(THEY look at each other a long moment. HE gently kisses her. A long kiss. THEY lie back on the bed.)

BARRY. (*Looking up suddenly.*) You know something? I think my pulse rate's gone up.

(GEN cuffs him affectionately.)

THE END

Also By

Roger Hall

GLIDE TIME
MIDDLE-AGE SPREAD
STATE OF THE PLAY
FIFTY FIFTY
MULTIPLE CHOICE
DREAM OF SUSSEX DOWNS
THE SHARE CLUB
AFTER THE CRASH

SAMUELFRENCH.COM

OTHER TITLES AVAILABLE FROM SAMUEL FRENCH

PERFECT WEDDING
Robin Hawdon

Comedy / 2m, 4f / Interior

A man wakes up in the bridal suite on his wedding morning to find an extremely attractive naked girl in bed beside him. In the depths of a stag night hangover, he can't even remember meeting her. Before he can get her out, his bride to be arrives to dress for the wedding. In the ensuing panic, the girl is locked in the bathroom. The best man is persuaded to claim her, but he gets confused and introduces the chamber maid to the bride as his date. The crisis escalates to nuclear levels by the time the mother of the bride and the best man's actual girlfriend arrive. This rare combination of riotous farce and touching love story has provoked waves of laughter across Europe and America.

"Laughs abound."
– *Wisconsin Advocate*

"The full house audience roared with delight."
– *Green Bay Gazette*

SAMUELFRENCH.COM

www.ingramcontent.com/pod-product-compliance
Lightning Source LLC
Chambersburg PA
CBHW070646300426
44111CB00013B/2294